September 23–October 22

Liberty Phi

LIBRA

INTRODUCTION

A strology is all about the planets in our skies and what energy and characteristics influence us. From ancient times, people have wanted to understand the rhythms of life and looked to the skies and their celestial bodies for inspiration, and the ancient constellations are there in the 12 zodiac signs we recognise from astrology. The Ancient Greeks devised narratives related to myths and legends about their celestial ancestors, to which they referred to make decisions and choices. Roman mythology did the same and over the years these ancient wisdoms became refined into today's modern astrology.

The configuration of the planets in the sky at the time and place of our birth is unique to each and every one of us, and what this means and how it plays out throughout our lives is both fascinating and informative. Just knowing which planet rules your sun sign is the beginning of an exploratory journey that can provide you with a useful tool for life.

Understanding the meaning, energetic nature and power of each planet, where this sits in your birth chart and what this might mean is all important information and linked to your date, place and time of birth, relevant *only* to you. Completely individual, the way in which you can work with the power of the planets comes from understanding their qualities and how this might influence the position in which they sit in your chart.

What knowledge of astrology can give you is the tools for working out how a planetary pattern might influence you, because of its relationship to your particular planetary configuration and circumstances. Each sun sign has a set of characteristics linked to its ruling planet – for example, Libra is ruled by Venus – and, in turn, to each of the 12 Houses (see page 81) that form the structure of every individual's birth chart (see page 78). Once you know the meanings of these and how these relate to different areas of your life, you can begin to work out what might be relevant to you when, for example, you read in a magazine horoscope that there's a Full Moon in Capricorn or that Jupiter is transiting Mars.

Each of the 12 astrological or zodiac sun signs is ruled by a planet (see page 52) and looking at a planet's characteristics will give you an indication of the influences brought to bear on each sign. It's useful to have a general understanding of these influences, because your birth chart includes many of them, in different house or planetary configurations, which gives you information about how uniquely *you* you are. Also included in this book are the minor planets (see page 102), also relevant to the information your chart provides.

LIBRA

Our sun sign is determined by the date of our birth wherever we are born, and if you are a Libra you were born between September 23rd and October 22nd. Bear in mind, however, that if you were born on one or other of those actual dates it's worth checking your *time* of birth, if you know it, against the year you were born and where. That's because no one is born 'on the cusp' (see page 78) and because there will be a moment on those days when Virgo shifts to Libra, and Libra shifts to Scorpio. It's well worth a check, especially if you've never felt quite convinced that the characteristics of your designated sun sign match your own.

The constellation of Libra, the Latin word for weighing scales, is one of the largest and takes the shape of a triangle with two extended lines. The Romans particularly favoured this constellation and its links to balance and harmony. The brightest star, Beta Librae or Zubeneschamali sits at the top, taking its name from the Arabic term for 'northern claw' because of its proximity to the constellation of Scorpio.

Libra is ruled by the Roman goddess Venus, so this sign embodies many of the qualities gifted by this planet, including a deep love and appreciation of beautiful things, and a gracious and elegant approach to life.

An air sign (like Gemini and Aquarius), Libra tends to show great flair in mental attitude, able to grasp facts and argue both sides. In fact, this ability to see everything in a balanced and rational way, and both sides of an argument, can give Libra the reputation for occasionally sitting on the fence. Their love of harmony often makes them disinclined to be the bad guy, so they may not always say exactly what they think or feel, tending to be diplomatic to a fault. Libra is also a cardinal sign, an action sign (like Aries, Cancer and Capricorn), and they like to get things done, so are quite capable of making unilateral decisions too. However, this tension between conciliation and action can sometimes create problems in Libra's inclination towards diplomacy.

The sign ♎ of Libra is taken originally from the Egyptian symbol for a setting sun, and within this context indicates the perfect balance between emotion and reason, which should be present in any partnership.

PHYSICAL POWER
Libra rules the lower back and the buttocks, and also that perfect pairing of two kidneys. Problems can arise from the lumbar region: low back pain that can be either muscular or spinal, and also kidney infections or stones.

SACRED GEMSTONE
The Opal, with its ethereal inner beauty, is Libra's stone and said to impart even greater wisdom to its wearer. It was also once considered the jewel of judges, able to influence the provision of justice.

OPPOSITE SIGN
Aries

Depicted by the Scales, Libra is often interpreted as the sign that seeks a balanced life, one of harmony and diplomacy. But all this emphasis on keeping the peace can come at a price and their occasional indecision or apparent fickleness can be a disappointment to lovers, family, friends or work colleagues. In fact, this commitment to avoiding conflict can mean giving away some of that Libra power, because sometimes it's essential to say 'no'.

Libra is also renowned for their charm. Ruling planet Venus brings all the charms of the zodiac to play, and never more so than when socialising, which many of this sign really love to do. Bringing people together for events is often done with flair and generosity, not least because Libra loves to get together with like-minded people with whom they can share their ideas. Nothing pleases them more than intellectually stimulating conversation over a meal in beautiful surroundings and many Libras have a real gift for bringing disparate groups of people together.

As an air sign, Libra also enjoys an audience for their ideas, and this can extend beyond socialising and into the workplace where they are very well equipped to negotiate. Here too they like to please and can go to some lengths to accommodate disparate groups to keep the peace and life harmonious. In fact, how they are seen is often very important to Libra, and unconsciously they often work hard to be admired and applauded for their efforts.

Libra is always happiest in a partnership of some sort, and actively seeks these out through their personal relationships, but also through work. With the right person this can be joyous, but because their motivation is sometimes a partnership at any price, Libra doesn't always make great decisions. Also, they can spend so long weighing up the pros and cons of a situation (or person) that the moment passes and is lost. It's as well for Libra to be aware of this trait, and exercise the rationality that many air signs benefit from to counter the inclination to facilitate too much.

In their approach to others, Libra is open-hearted, but in the same way that they want to be seen well, there is a tendency to judge others on how *they* are seen. If someone is beautifully turned out and dressed, Libra's appreciation can be rather superficial and they may find that others are not entirely as they seem. They could do well to take a leaf out of their opposite sign Aries' more intuitive take on life and not to be so quick to judge by appearance. The beauty of Libra is that as they mature they are able to learn from experience how to balance some of these traits in themselves, and overcome some of the difficulties that can undermine them.

THE MOON IN
YOUR CHART

While your zodiac sign is your sun sign, making you a sun sign Libra, the Moon also plays a role in your birth chart and if you know the time and place of your birth, along with your birth date, you can get your birth chart done (see page 78). From this you can discover in which zodiac sign your Moon is positioned in your chart.

The Moon reflects the characteristics of who you are at the time of your birth, your innate personality, how you express yourself and how you are seen by others. This is in contrast to our sun sign, which indicates the more dominant characteristics we reveal as we travel through life. The Moon also represents the feminine in our natal chart (the Sun the masculine) and the sign in which our Moon falls can indicate how we express the feminine side of our personality. Looking at the two signs together in our charts immediately creates a balance.

MOON IN LIBRA

The Moon spends roughly 2.5 days in each zodiac sign as it moves through all 12 signs during its monthly cycle. This means that the Moon is regularly in Libra, and it can be useful to know when this occurs and in particular when we have a New Moon or a Full Moon in Libra because these are especially good times for you to focus your energy and intentions.

A New Moon is always the start of a new cycle, an opportunity to set new intentions for the coming month, and when this is in your own sign, Libra, you can benefit from this additional energy and support. The Full Moon is an opportunity to reflect on the culmination of your earlier intentions.

NEW MOON
IN LIBRA AFFIRMATION

'I look to the beauty of the skies to nourish me,
renew my energy and to help me focus on
my intention, particularly where my relationships
are concerned.'

FULL MOON
IN LIBRA AFFIRMATION

'I look to find the balance in the culmination of
my intention, looking towards greater purpose and
realisation in my relationships.'

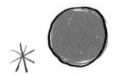

LIBRA HEALTH

The lower back is, almost literally, often the seat of Libra's health problems, with the lumbar area of the spine being a weak spot and occasionally at risk. Weak butt muscles, often from too much sitting, can also aggravate the lower back and make it more susceptible, so exercise that helps strengthen muscles to support the spinal joints is often recommended for Libra.

General exercise that keeps the body in good shape is a plus for Libra, who can be somewhat overindulgent from time to time when it comes to their diet, which naturally increases their girth. Team sports don't generally appeal to the non-competitive among Libra, although playing tennis or other sports in a partnership might. Walking is always good and easily factored into most people's daily routine, but Libra would also benefit from some specific exercise to improve their muscle tone and core strength, which in turn helps support the spinal joints of the lumbar region. Pilates in particular would be a good form of exercise, because it focuses on the core while building strength. It also helps improve posture and that in turn helps support the lower back.

POWER UP
YOUR LIBRA
ENERGY

There are often moments or periods when we feel uninspired, demotivated and low in energy. At these times it's worth working with your innate sun sign energy to power up again, and paying attention to what Libra relishes and needs can help support both physical and mental health.

As an air sign, Libra can have a tendency to overthink and ruminate, especially when constantly reviewing the pros and cons of a situation. This can become draining and completely exhausting. With Libra it's usually overdoing this aspect of life that can deplete energy, partly because when someone is ruminating on things to the exclusion of decision-making, they find it difficult to focus and get things done. For an action sign like Libra, this is extremely demotivating.

It's all too easy to get bogged down in life's trials and tribulations, to begin to find things overwhelming, and this can build over time without Libra even realising it. Exercise can really help here and a daily walk around the block, or through a park or green space with exposure to the natural world, can do a great deal to shift perspective. Just a change of light and scenery and exposure to the physical experience of fresh air, which enables Libra to breathe more calmly and reflect on things outside themselves, can really help. In addition, being physical in one form or another helps to lighten their mood through the production of endorphins in the brain.

Attention to diet can also help re-energise a depleted system, especially with Libra if they have a habit of overindulging in a calorie-rich diet. Switching to complex carbohydrates like brown rice and oats, plenty of fresh fruit and vegetables like apples, apricots, leafy green kale and sweet potatoes, and protein sources such as lean meat, tofu and fish can help replenish the body. Avoiding alcohol and highly caffeinated drinks will help reduce acidity in the body too. As ever with Libra, balance is key, and an avoidance of fatty, sugary or acid-producing foods, particularly those high in sodium, will also help protect the kidneys, an occasional weak spot for some Libras.

Herbs like parsley and mint are cleansing, alkalising and re-balancing, plus sweet spices like cardamom and cinnamon can be used instead of sugars, to improve flavours and pique the appetite without adding the pounds.

Utilise a New Moon in Libra with a ritual to set your intentions and power up: light a candle, use essential oil of cardamom to soothe your mood and concentration (this oil blends well with rose and uplifting ylang ylang), focus your thoughts on the change you wish to see and allow time to meditate on this. Place your gemstone (see page 13) in the moonlight. Write down your intentions and keep in a safe place. Meditate on the New Moon in Libra affirmation (see page 21).

At a Full Moon in Libra you will have the benefit of the Sun's reflected light to help illuminate what is working for you and what you can let go, because the Full Moon brings clarity.Take the time to meditate on the Full Moon in Libra affirmation (see page 21). Light a candle, place your gemstone in the moonlight and make a note of your thoughts and feelings, strengthened by the Moon in your sign.

LIBRA'S
SPIRITUAL
HOME

K nowing where to go to replenish your soul and recharge
your batteries both physically and spiritually is important
and worth serious consideration. For some Libras, their
spiritual home will always be the home which they have created
in partnership with another, rather than a geographical location.

But wherever they hail from, there are also a number of
countries where Libra will feel comfortable, whether they choose
to go there to live, work or just take a holiday. These locations are
as diverse as Burma and the Argentine, Japan, Fiji and Siberia. All
resonate with the mental energy that Libra finds so stimulating and
where they tend to seek out areas of beauty, both rural and urban,
in which to flourish.

Cities that also sparkle for Libra, whether to live or in which
to take a reinvigorating break, include Frankfurt, Cartagena, Vienna,
Chicago and Copenhagen. Libra doesn't tend to travel solo, but
when it's necessary there's some solace in places that resonate
with beauty and intellectual energy, in which they can prosper.

LIBRA
WOMAN

There's a certain elegance about many Libra women that's difficult to miss. Highly individual, they're capable of pairing exactly the right shoes with their outfit, or earrings with a scarf, their style unobtrusive but noticeable. It's as if Libra woman has taken to heart the Coco Chanel quote, 'Dress shabbily, they notice the dress; dress impeccably, they notice the woman,' because she does get noticed and it's not because of any designer label or bling. That's how Libra woman prefers to go through life, understated but definitely not underestimated.

Ruled by Venus, Libra's appreciation for beauty extends beyond their own self-presentation; they also look for it in their surroundings, and even the way in which they organise themselves can be something of an art form. From desk to kitchen cabinet, it would be typical of Libra women to make them aesthetically interesting in some way. She certainly likes her surroundings to be personally pleasing and generally goes to some effort to ensure a suitable ambience, whether in her workplace or bedroom, in which she can flourish mentally.

In company, Libra woman is often a very good listener, not least because she likes to weigh up the pros and cons of any argument presented to her before deciding what to say, and because of this her advice is often sought. She's likely to particularly relish one-to-one conversations, driving intimacy through intense conversations. Finding an intellectual kindred spirit is very important to most Libra women, whether as a friend or a lover, because without that spark that generates a flame, there's little to keep her interested.

That's not to say she's incapable of light-hearted exchange; in fact, this air sign revels in it, often artfully playing devil's advocate to provoke a flirtatious moment. It's an attractive feature, this witty repartee, but sometimes it's used as a defence and she can be misunderstood as a consequence. Its downside is that some may find her verbal dexterity fickle, and fail to consider her as a serious contender whether in friendship, love or at work.

LIBRA MAN

There's an easy charm to many Libra men that marks them out in a crowd. He's the man with a social bent, often looking to elevate the discussion and raise it above bar-room banter into a more interesting exchange, which is typical of all the air signs. But he actively seeks out the opportunity to address and weigh up a point, interested in the arguments and counterarguments that might be brought to bear. This can be wonderfully effective if he's a legal brain at work, but sometimes it's good to tone this down in a social setting.

Luckily, there's enough self-awareness in most Libra men to realise you attract more flies with honey than vinegar, and they can be capable of literally flicking a switch to turn on the charm (although they are also often equally capable of switching it off again rather abruptly). This trait often plays very well to their general relationships, easing social or work situations, but when it comes to the more lasting of partnerships that many Libra men crave, it's as well to find a little more authenticity and integrity to avoid being dismissed as unreliable or fickle.

Generally Libra men are well turned out, with the sort of attention to detail often seen in Taurus men, also ruled by Venus. There's a love of quality which means they may well own several high-end, handmade shirts or bespoke suits in preference to a wardrobe stuffed with inferior items. And you're more likely to find a pair of handmade shoes on the feet of a Libra than possibly any other sun sign! They love quality and luxury if they can afford it, and will often flaunt it.

They may not be by nature instinctively the most practical of men because Libra's inclination is towards more cerebral talents, but they have the ability to make a good effort of most of what they apply themselves to because they take care to find out the facts first. This is often one of Libra man's unrecognised qualities, making flat-pack furniture assembly, for example, a surprising forte until you remember that this is a sign that likes to balance knowledge with application, intellectual capacity with practical skills.

LIBRA IN LOVE

Ruled by Venus, the goddess of love, the amorous nature of Libra is very seductive, alluring and charming. They tend to surpass all other signs when it comes to making their love obvious to a prospective partner and a first date is probably no exception. This is the sign of luxury too, so Libra in love may try to attract through gifts or other lovely treats. Or, at least, the promise of them. Libra really does want to share romantic trips to Paris, delicious meals at expensive restaurants, or shopping trips to high-end stores, and this can sometimes be the currency of their charm – which, unfortunately, may not always be realised. In order not to be considered untrustworthy, Libra may need to learn to reign in their seductive promises.

Libra also rules the 7th House of partnerships (see page 84), so this is a sun sign that is positively committed to the idea of being in partnership, including the partnership that arises from intimate relationships and can result in marriage. And because they instinctively look for the balance in any situation, Libra will do this in love too.

LIBRA AS
A LOVER

There's a refinement to Libra's sensuality, even in the most virile of the male of the species, which tends to set them apart. This is a sign that loves the flirtation, seductive ploys and foreplay that leads to consummation in a relationship, as can be expected by those ruled by Venus, goddess of love. Libra lovers are ultimately looking for a partnership and even though they are prepared to date and have fun along the way, they're more likely than some signs to call a halt early on if it doesn't seem to them to be heading towards that end goal.

But Libra is also a cardinal sign, so prefers to take action to achieve their goals, in love as well as in any other area of their life. What sometimes results from this combination of an air and cardinal sign, can be a whiff of calculation: the charm, the planning, the thinking through, the action. It's almost as if there's a script that needs to be adhered to, so the first thing that Libra can do to improve as a lover is to learn a little spontaneity and reciprocity, because love is a two-way, give-and-take, process.

And just occasionally, this tension in Libra can result in an over-fastidious take on love, when in fact the romance needs to weave its own magic and allow Libra to fully express themselves sexually and harmoniously in partnership with another. If they allow their intellectual brain to inhibit their more erotic inclinations, Libra can miss out, so learning to 'let go' is useful for this occasionally sexually uptight sign. Libra knows intellectually that it's something that can often be explored through physical intimacy, and even if they can't yet tick all the boxes in a relationship, they need to trust that deep love and commitment sometimes evolves more easily from this proximity.

WHAT'S IN LIBRA'S BEDSIDE CABINET?

A bottle of vintage champagne to share and loosen those inhibitions

A collected edition of erotic love poetry

Blue silk blindfold and wrist ties

WHICH SIGN
SUITS LIBRA?

In relationships with Libra, the sun sign of the other person and the ruling planet of that sign can bring out the best, or sometimes the worst, in a lover. Knowing what might spark, smoulder or suffocate love is worth closer investigation, but always remember that sun sign astrology is only a starting point for any relationship.

LIBRA
AND ARIES

Opposing partners but both are
cardinal action signs which kindles
an initial spark, and of course their
ruling planets Venus and Mars
epitomise a love match. But there
can sometimes be a power struggle
that can undermine the balance
that Libra seeks.

LIBRA AND
TAURUS

Two planets ruled by Venus, but there's
a subtle difference in their expression
and Libra's air can find Taurus' earthy
side restrictive. However, there is
a natural harmony between the two
that can ease any tension, making
this a happy union.

LIBRA AND
GEMINI

A tricky pairing between two signs
with an equal tendency to be rather
airy in their approach, while the
pairing of Venus with Mercury can
aggravate any sense of the fickle
between them, and the initial spark
can easily burn out.

♎

LIBRA AND CANCER

At first Venus can be captivated by the Moon, but Cancer's emotional side can sometimes irritate Libra's more fastidious approach to the intellect, even while they enjoy the balance this sign can bring to any partnership.

LIBRA AND LEO

Libra often falls for exuberant Leo, ruled by the sun, illuminating all before them with the sort of creative generosity on which Venus can thrive – as long as the lion doesn't try to dominate, because balance is everything to the scales.

LIBRA AND VIRGO

There's a fastidiousness about Virgo that chimes with Libra. They both like to think things through, but in this capacity Mercury can sometimes irritate Venus if they are too dogmatic and unprepared to see both sides of the coin every time.

LIBRA AND LIBRA

They certainly understand each other's traits better than anyone, and this should help them harmonise. But sometimes being too similar means there's no element of surprise or difference that helps pique interest and keeps a relationship fresh.

LIBRA AND SCORPIO

Libra's Venus tends to be intellectually fascinated by Pluto's transformational depths, and if this relationship has enough of Libra's air to balance Scorpio's watery intensity, this partnership is often very harmonious.

LIBRA AND SAGITTARIUS

Expansive planet Jupiter, with its eye on the horizon, may not give Venus the attention they feel is their due, even while Libra's air fires up Sagittarius, so it's up to them whether this will make it through the early stages to a lasting partnership.

LIBRA AND CAPRICORN

Libra really appreciates the stability that Capricorn can bring, helping stop the scales from wobbling with big Saturn energy, while Venus' charms are very seductive to the goat, whose earthiness sometimes needs a little lightening up.

LIBRA AND AQUARIUS

Air and air produce lots of intellectual harmony, but in two very different ways and Libra can find that unpredictable Uranus is rather too challenging unless suitably charmed by diplomatic Venus to achieve the balance they crave.

LIBRA AND PISCES

Pisces' imaginative, dreamy Neptune can be very attractive to Libra's Venus, creating a real balance to all that intellect and allowing them to dream a little more freely. As long as there are boundaries, this can be a very fruitful pairing.

LIBRA AT WORK

When it comes to careers, Libra tends to gravitate towards those jobs that require people skills and intellectual problem-solving, although many have a deep love of art that finds them seeking expression through this medium in some way. Their desire for balance in all things may attract them to gymnastics or ballet, where they can achieve this physically as well as intellectually.

While many teachers are Libra, striving to keep the peace in a classroom, or Human Resources managers, trying to match employers to jobs and negotiate employment law, Libra seeks interest and diversity in whatever they choose to do. In fact, law itself is an attractive career or workplace for those whose astrological sign is the symbol of justice, with its commitment to fairness and truth. In many ways this is more important to them than remuneration, although most Libras make a good living whatever their choice of career.

Negotiators at heart, this is often born from Libra's desire to avoid confrontation, but this doesn't always solve the problem. In an effort to see both sides, Libra sometimes vacillates in their decision-making, because they sometimes find the process difficult. Endlessly weighing up the pros and cons of a situation in order to be *sure* that the best outcome is achieved, can often hinder them. This is where maturity is Libra's friend and as their action trait helps them grow in life experience and confidence, this process becomes easier. And they also learn that you can't please all the people, all the time.

While they generally prefer to work in partnership in some way, Libra is capable of working independently or in a freelance capacity, especially if they are able to flex their muscles in areas that engage them intellectually and they have the capacity for – for example, freelance journalism. This can arise out of a complementary area of interest like the arts, and many Venus-ruled signs have an appreciation of art in its many guises.

LIBRA AT HOME

The same balance and harmony that Libra seeks through their profession, they also seek at home. In fact, as long as they can achieve this at home, generally with another, then they are happy. And domestic happiness isn't something that Libra takes for granted. Of all the signs, they are the most likely to accept it requires give and take and are happy to both anticipate this necessity and work towards it.

Libra likes to avoid confrontation so is usually more than happy to take on necessary chores without complaint. Plus, they like their home to look attractive and, although not the most practical of the signs, they will learn how to paint and decorate if necessary. Of course, there are exceptions to this rule, but it's a rare Libra that can ignore the dirty crockery sitting in a washing-up bowl for long. This makes Libra valued as housemates in whatever relationship they are to the rest of the household.

It's not unusual to find that Libra has created their own personal space within a home. This may be an extensive library of well-loved books or just a corner in which they've created an attractive nook or workspace with a pleasing view to sit and relax or work. Libra aren't particularly possessive about what they own, but they do take real pleasure in beautiful things, whether this is a piece of art or beautiful sculpture or floral arrangement to aid thoughtful contemplation.

The extension of their home into an open space, enabling them to look out at the sky, is something many Libras instinctively seek. As an air sign, Libra loves to feel the air resonate beyond them, inspiring their own vision and thoughts, bringing harmony into the home. And even though many Libras can live happily alone, their inclination is to share their home with those of a similar vision.

FREE THE
SPIRIT

Understanding your own sun sign astrology is only part of the picture. It provides you with a template to examine and reflect on your own life's journey but also the context for this through your relationships with others, intimate or otherwise, and within the culture and environment in which you live.

Throughout time, the Sun and planets of our universe have kept to their paths and astrologers have used this ancient wisdom to understand the pattern of the universe. In this way, astrology is a tool to utilise these wisdoms, a way of helping make sense of the energies we experience as the planets shift in our skies.

'A physician without a knowledge of astrology has no right to call himself a physician,' said Hippocrates, the Greek physician born in 460 BC, who understood better than anyone how these psychic energies worked. As did Carl Jung, the 20th-century philosopher and psychoanalyst, because he said, 'Astrology represents the summation of all the psychological knowledge of antiquity.'

THE 10
PLANETS

SUN

Although the Sun is officially a star, for the purpose of astrology it's considered a planet. It is also the centre of our universe and gives us both light and energy; our lives are dependent on it and it embodies our creative life force. As a life giver, the Sun is considered a masculine entity, the patriarch and ruler of the skies. Our sun sign is where we start our astrological journey whichever sign it falls in, and as long as we know which day of which month we were born, we have this primary knowledge.

MOON

We now know that the Moon is actually a natural satellite of the Earth (the third planet from the Sun) rather than a planet but is considered such for the purposes of astrology. It's dependent on the Sun for its reflected light, and it is only through their celestial relationship that we can see it. In this way, the Moon in each of our birth charts depicts the feminine energy to balance the masculine Sun's life force, the ying to its yang. It is not an impotent or subservient presence, particularly when you consider how it gives the world's oceans their tides, the relentless energy of the ebb and flow powering up the seas. The Moon's energy also helps illuminate our unconscious desires, helping to bring these to the service of our self-knowledge.

MERCURY

RULES THE ASTROLOGICAL SIGNS OF GEMINI AND VIRGO

Mercury, messenger of the gods, has always been associated with speed and agility, whether in body or mind. Because of this, Mercury is considered to be the planet of quick wit and anything requiring verbal dexterity and the application of intelligence. Those with Mercury prominent in their chart love exchanging and debating ideas and telling stories (often with a tendency to embellish the truth of a situation), making them prominent in professions where these qualities are valuable.

Astronomically, Mercury is the closest planet to the Sun and moves around a lot in our skies. What's also relevant is that several times a year Mercury appears to be retrograde (see page 99) which has the effect of slowing down or disrupting its influence.

VENUS

The goddess of beauty, love and pleasure. Venus is
the second planet from the Sun and benefits from
this proximity, having received its positive vibes.
Depending on which astrological sign Venus falls in
your chart will influence how you relate to art and
culture and the opposite sex. The characteristics of
this sign will tell you all you need to know about
what you aspire to, where you seek and how you
experience pleasure, along with the types of lover you
attract. Again, partly depending on where it's placed,
Venus can sometimes increase self-indulgence which
can be a less positive aspect of a hedonistic life.

MARS

RULES THE ASTROLOGICAL SIGN OF ARIES

This big, powerful planet is fourth from the Sun
and exerts an energetic force, powering up the
characteristics of the astrological sign in which it
falls in your chart. This will tell you how you assert
yourself, whether your anger flares or smoulders,
what might stir your passion and how you express
your sexual desires. Mars will show you what works
best for you to turn ideas into action, the sort of
energy you might need to see something through
and how your independent spirit can be most
effectively engaged.

JUPITER

Big, bountiful Jupiter is the largest planet in our solar system and fifth from the Sun. It heralds optimism, generosity and general benevolence. Whichever sign Jupiter falls in in your chart is where you will find the characteristics for your particular experience of luck, happiness and good fortune. Jupiter will show you which areas to focus on to gain the most and best from your life. Wherever Jupiter appears in your chart it will bring a positive influence and when it's prominent in our skies we all benefit.

SATURN

Saturn is considered akin to Old Father Time, with
all the patience, realism and wisdom that archetype
evokes. Sometimes called the taskmaster of the skies,
its influence is all about how we handle responsibility
and it requires that we graft and apply ourselves in
order to learn life's lessons. The sixth planet from the
Sun, Saturn's 'return' (see page 100) to its place in an
individual's birth chart occurs approximately every
28 years. How self-disciplined you are about
overcoming opposition or adversity will be
influenced by the characteristics of the sign in which
this powerful planet falls in your chart.

URANUS

The seventh planet from the Sun, Uranus is the planet of unpredictability, change and surprise, and whether you love or loathe the impact of Uranus will depend in part on which astrological sign it influences in your chart. How you respond to its influence is entirely up to the characteristics of the sign it occupies in your chart. Whether you see the change it heralds as a gift or a curse is up to you, but because it takes seven years to travel through a sign, its presence in a sign can influence a generation.

NEPTUNE

Neptune ruled the sea, and this planet is all about deep waters of mystery, imagination and secrets. It's also representative of our spiritual side so the characteristics of whichever astrological sign it occupies in your chart will influence how this plays out in your life. Neptune is the eighth planet from the Sun and its influence can be subtle and mysterious. The astrological sign in which it falls in your chart will indicate how you realise your vision, dream and goals. The only precaution is if it falls in an equally watery sign, creating a potential difficulty in distinguishing between fantasy and reality.

PLUTO

RULES THE ASTROLOGICAL SIGN OF SCORPIO

Pluto is the furthest planet from the Sun and exerts a regenerative energy that transforms but often requires destruction to erase what's come before in order to begin again. Its energy often lies dormant and then erupts, so the astrological sign in which it falls will have a bearing on how this might play out in your chart. Transformation can be very positive but also very painful. When Pluto's influence is strong, change occurs and how you react or respond to this will be very individual. Don't fear it, but reflect on how to use its energy to your benefit.

YOUR SUN SIGN

Your sun or zodiac sign is the one in which you were born, determined by the date of your birth. Your sun sign is ruled by a specific planet. For example, Libra is ruled by Venus but Capricorn by Saturn, so we already have the first piece of information and the first piece of our individual jigsaw puzzle.

The next piece of the jigsaw is understanding that the energy of a particular planet in your birth chart (see page 78) plays out via the characteristics of the astrological sign in which it's positioned, and this is hugely valuable in understanding some of the patterns of your life. You may have your Sun in Libra, and a good insight into the characteristics of this sign, but what if you have Neptune in Leo? Or Venus in Aries? Uranus in Virgo? Understanding the impact of these influences can help you reflect on the way you react or respond and the choices you can make, helping to ensure more positive outcomes.

If, for example, with Uranus in Taurus you are resistant to change, remind yourself that change is inevitable and can be positive, allowing you to work with it rather than against its influence. If you have Neptune in Virgo, it will bring a more spiritual element to this practical earth sign, while Mercury in Aquarius will enhance the predictive element of your analysis and judgement. The scope and range and useful aspect of having this knowledge is just the beginning of how you can utilise astrology to live your best life.

PLANETS IN TRANSIT

In addition, the planets do not stay still. They are said to transit (move) through the course of an astrological year. Those closest to us, like Mercury, transit quite regularly (every 88 days), while those further away, like Pluto, take much longer, in this case 248 years to come full circle. So the effects of each planet can vary depending on their position and this is why we hear astrologers talk about someone's Saturn return (see page 100), Mercury retrograde (see page 99) or about Capricorn (or other sun sign) 'weather'. This is indicative of an influence that can be anticipated and worked with and is both universal and personal. The shifting positions of the planets bring an influence to bear on each of us, linked to the position of our own planetary influences and how these have a bearing on each other. If you understand the nature of these planetary influences you can begin to work with, rather than against, them and this information can be very much to your benefit.

First, though, you need to take a look at the component parts of astrology, the pieces of your personal jigsaw, then you'll have the information you need to make sense of how your sun sign might be affected during the changing patterns of the planets.

YOUR BIRTH CHART

With the date, time and place of birth, you can easily find out
where your (or anyone else's) planets are positioned from an online
astrological chart programme (see page 110). This will give you an
exact sun sign position, which you probably already know, but it
can also be useful if you think you were born 'on the cusp' because
it will give you an *exact* indication of what sign you were born in.
In addition, this natal chart will tell you your Ascendant sign, which
sign your Moon is in, along with the other planets specific to your
personal and completely individual chart and the Houses (see page
81) in which the astrological signs are positioned.

A birth chart is divided into 12 sections, representing each of
the 12 Houses (see pages 82–85) with your Ascendant or Rising sign
always positioned in the 1st House, and the other 11 Houses running
counter-clockwise from one to 12.

♎

ASCENDANT OR RISING SIGN

Your Ascendant is a first, important part of the complexity of an individual birth chart. While your sun sign gives you an indication of the personality you will inhabit through the course of your life, it is your Ascendant or Rising sign – which is the sign rising at the break of dawn on the Eastern horizon at the time and on the date of your birth – that often gives a truer indication of how you will project your personality and consequently how the world sees you. So even though you were born a sun sign Libra, whatever sign your Ascendant is in, for example Cancer, will be read through the characteristics of this astrological sign.

Your Ascendant is always in your 1st House, which is the House of the Self (see page 82) and the other houses always follow the same consecutive astrological order. So if, for example, your Ascendant is Leo, then your second house is in Virgo, your third house in Libra, and so on. Each house has its own characteristics but how these will play out in your individual chart will be influenced by the sign positioned in it.

Opposite your Ascendant is your Descendant sign, positioned in the 7th House (see page 84) and this shows what you look for in a partnership, your complementary 'other half' as it were. There's always something intriguing about what the Descendant can help us to understand, and it's worth knowing yours and being on the lookout for it when considering a long-term marital or business partnership.

THE
12
HOUSES

While each of the 12 Houses represent different aspects of our lives, they are also ruled by one of the 12 astrological signs, giving each house its specific characteristics. When we discover, for example, that we have Capricorn in the 12th House, this might suggest a pragmatic or practical approach to spirituality. Or, if you had Gemini in your 6th House, this might suggest a rather airy approach to organisation.

1ST HOUSE

RULED BY ARIES

The first impression you give walking into a room, how you like to be seen, your sense of self and the energy with which you approach life.

2ND HOUSE

RULED BY TAURUS

What you value, including what you own that provides your material security; your self-value and work ethic, how you earn your income.

3RD HOUSE

RULED BY GEMINI

How you communicate through words, deeds and gestures; also how you learn and function in a group, including within your own family.

4 TH HOUSE

RULED BY CANCER

This is about your home, your security
and how you take care of yourself and
your family; and also about those family
traditions you hold dear.

5 TH HOUSE

RULED BY LEO

Creativity in all its forms, including fun
and eroticism, intimate relationships and
procreation, self-expression
and positive fulfilment.

6 TH HOUSE

RULED BY VIRGO

How you organise your daily routine, your
health, your business affairs, and how you
are of service to others, from those
in your family to the workplace.

7TH HOUSE

RULED BY LIBRA

This is about partnerships and shared
goals, whether marital or in business,
and what we look for in these to
complement ourselves.

8TH HOUSE

RULED BY SCORPIO

Regeneration, through death and rebirth,
and also our legacy and how this might be
realised through sex, procreation
and progeny.

9TH HOUSE

RULED BY SAGITTARIUS

Our world view, cultures outside our
own and the bigger picture beyond our
immediate horizon, to which we travel
either in body or mind.

10TH HOUSE

RULED BY CAPRICORN

Our aims and ambitions in life, what we aspire
to and what we're prepared to do to achieve it;
this is how we approach our working lives.

11TH HOUSE

RULED BY AQUARIUS

The house of humanity and our
friendships, our relationships with the
wider world, our tribe or group to which
we feel an affiliation.

12TH HOUSE

RULED BY PISCES

Our spiritual side resides here. Whether this
is religious or not, it embodies our inner life,
beliefs and the deeper connections we forge.

THE FOUR
ELEMENTS

The 12 astrological signs are divided into four groups, representing the four elements: fire, water, earth and air. This gives each of the three signs in each group additional characteristics.

FIRE

ARIES ❧ LEO ❧ SAGITTARIUS

Embodying warmth, spontaneity and enthusiasm.

♎ LIBRA

WATER

CANCER ❖ SCORPIO ❖ PISCES

Embodying a more feeling, spiritual and intuitive side.

EARTH

TAURUS ∾ VIRGO ∾ CAPRICORN

Grounded and sure-footed and sometimes rather stubborn.

♎

AIR

GEMINI ❧ LIBRA ❧ AQUARIUS

Flourishing in the world of vision, ideas and perception.

FIXED, CARDINAL OR MUTABLE?

The 12 signs are further divided into three groups of four, giving additional characteristics of being fixed, cardinal or mutable. These represent the way in which they respond to situations.

FIXED

TAURUS, LEO, SCORPIO AND AQUARIUS ARE FIXED SIGNS

Their energy tends to be steady and they are less
reactive, more responsive, although they can have
a tendency to be resistant to change and need
encouragement.

CARDINAL

ARIES, CANCER, LIBRA AND CAPRICORN ARE CARDINAL SIGNS

Their energy is often instinctive and action-oriented,
enabling them to get things started, although there's
sometimes a tendency to fail to carry things through.

MUTABLE

GEMINI, VIRGO, SAGITTARIUS AND PISCES ARE MUTABLE SIGNS

The clue here is their adaptability and responsiveness to
change, which they don't fear, and readiness to listen to
and embrace new ideas.

MERCURY RETROGRADE

This occurs several times over the astrological year and lasts for around four weeks, with a shadow week either side (a quick Google search will tell you the forthcoming dates). It's important what sign Mercury is in while it's retrograde, because its impact will be affected by the characteristics of that sign. For example, if Mercury is retrograde in Gemini, the sign of communication that is ruled by Mercury, the effect will be keenly felt in all areas of communication. However, if Mercury is retrograde in Aquarius, which rules the house of friendships and relationships, this may keenly affect our communication with large groups, or if in Sagittarius, which rules the house of travel, it could affect travel itineraries and encourage us to check our documents carefully.

Mercury retrograde can also be seen as an opportunity to pause, review or reconsider ideas and plans, to regroup, recalibrate and recuperate, and generally to take stock of where we are and how we might proceed. In our fast-paced 24/7 lives, Mercury retrograde can often be a useful opportunity to slow down and allow ourselves space to restore some necessary equilibrium.

SATURN RETURN

When the planet Saturn returns to the place in your chart that it occupied at the time of your birth, it has an impact. This occurs roughly every 28 years, so we can see immediately that it correlates with ages that we consider representative of different life stages and when we might anticipate change or adjustment to a different era. At 28 we can be considered at full adult maturity, probably established in our careers and relationships, maybe with children; at 56 we have reached middle age and are possibly at another of life's crossroads; and at 84, we might be considered at the full height of our wisdom, our lives almost complete. If you know the time and place of your birth date, an online Saturn return calculator can give you the exact timing.

It will also be useful to identify in which astrological sign Saturn falls in your chart, which will help you reflect on its influence, as both influences can be very illuminating about how you will experience and manage the impact of its return. Often the time leading up to a personal Saturn return is a demanding one, but the lessons learnt help inform the decisions made about how to progress your own goals. Don't fear this period, but work with its influence: knowledge is power and Saturn has a powerful energy you can harness should you choose.

THE MINOR PLANETS

Sun sign astrology seldom makes mention of these 'minor' planets that also orbit the Sun, but increasingly their subtle influence is being referenced. If you have had your birth chart done (if you know your birth time and place you can do this online) you will have access to this additional information.

Like the 10 main planets on the previous pages, these 18 minor entities will also be positioned in an astrological sign, bringing their energy to bear on these characteristics. You may, for example, have Fortuna in Leo, or Diana in Sagittarius. Look to these for their subtle influences on your birth chart and life via the sign they inhabit, all of which will serve to animate and resonate further the information you can reference on your own personal journey.

AESCULAPIA

Jupiter's grandson and a powerful
healer, Aesculapia was taught by
Chiron and influences us in what
could be life-saving action, realised
through the characteristics of the sign
in which it falls in our chart.

BACCHUS

Jupiter's son, Bacchus is similarly
benevolent but can sometimes lack
restraint in the pursuit of pleasure.
How this plays out in your chart
is dependent on the sign in which
it falls.

APOLLO

Jupiter's son, gifted in art, music and
healing, Apollo rides the Sun across
the skies. His energy literally lights up
the way in which you inspire others,
characterised by the sign in which it
falls in your chart.

CERES

Goddess of agriculture and mother of
Proserpina, Ceres is associated with
the seasons and how we manage cycles
of change in our lives. This energy is
influenced by the sign in which it falls
in our chart.

CHIRON

Teacher of the gods, Chiron knew all about healing herbs and medical practices and he lends his energy to how we tackle the impossible or the unthinkable, that which seems difficult to do.

DIANA

Jupiter's independent daughter was allowed to run free without the shackles of marriage. Where this falls in your birth chart will indicate what you are not prepared to sacrifice in order to conform.

CUPID

Son of Venus. The sign into which Cupid falls will influence how you inspire love and desire in others, not always appropriately and sometimes illogically but it can still be an enduring passion.

FORTUNA

Jupiter's daughter, who is always shown blindfolded, influences your fated role in other people's lives, how you show up for them without really understanding why, and at the right time.

HYGEIA

Daughter of Aesculapia and also associated with health, Hygeia is about how you anticipate risk and the avoidance of unwanted outcomes. The way you do this is characterised by the sign in which Hygeia falls.

MINERVA

Another of Jupiter's daughters, depicted by an owl, will show you via the energy given to a particular astrological sign in your chart how you show up at your most intelligent and smart. How you operate intellectually.

JUNO

Juno was the wife of Jupiter and her position in your chart will indicate where you will make a commitment in order to feel safe and secure. It's where you might seek protection in order to flourish.

OPS

The wife of Saturn, Ops saved the life of her son Jupiter by giving her husband a stone to eat instead of him. Her energy in our chart enables us to find positive solutions to life's demands and dilemmas.

PANACEA

Gifted with healing powers, Panacea provides us with a remedy for all ills and difficulties, and how this plays out in your life will depend on the characteristics of the astrological sign in which her energy falls.

PSYCHE

Psyche, Venus' daughter-in-law, shows us that part of ourselves that is easy to love and endures through adversity, and your soul that survives death and flies free, like the butterfly that depicts her.

PROSERPINA

Daughter of Ceres, abducted by Pluto, Proserpina has to spend her life divided between earth and the underworld and she represents how we bridge the gulf between different and difficult aspects of our lives.

SALACIA

Neptune's wife, Salacia stands on the seashore bridging land and sea, happily bridging the two realities. In your chart, she shows how you can harmoniously bring two sides of yourself together.

VESTA

Daughter of Saturn, Vesta's job was to protect Rome and in turn she was protected by vestal virgins. Her energy influences how we manage our relationships with competitive females and male authority figures.

VULCAN

Vulcan was a blacksmith who knew how to control fire and fashion metal into shape, and through the sign in which it falls in your chart will show you how you control your passion and make it work for you.

FURTHER READING

Jung's Studies in Astrology: Prophecies, Magic and the Qualities of Time,

Liz Greene, Routledge (2018)

Lunar Oracle: Harness the Power of the Moon,

Liberty Phi, OH Editions (2021)

Metaphysics of Astrology: Why Astrology Works,

Ivan Antic, Independently published (2020)

*Parkers' Astrology: The Definitive Guide to Using Astrology in Every Aspect
of Your Life,*

Julia and Derek Parker, Dorling Kindersley (2020)

USEFUL WEBSITES

Alicebellastrology.com
Astro.com
Astrology.com
Cafeastrology.com
Costarastrology.com
Jessicaadams.com

USEFUL APPS

Astro Future
Co-Star
Moon
Sanctuary
Time Nomad
Time Passages

ACKNOWLEDGEMENTS

Thanks are due to my Taurean publisher Kate Pollard for commissioning this Astrology Oracle series, to Piscean Matt Tomlinson for his careful editing, and to Evi O Studio for their beautiful design and illustrations.

ABOUT THE AUTHOR

As a sun sign Aquarius Liberty Phi loves to explore the world and has lived on three different continents, currently residing in North America. Their Gemini moon inspires them to communicate their love of astrology and other esoteric practices while Leo rising helps energise them. Their first publication, also released by OH Editions, is a box set of 36 oracle cards and accompanying guide, entitled *Lunar Oracle: Harness the Power of the Moon*.

Published in 2023 by OH Editions,
an imprint of Welbeck Non-Fiction Ltd,
part of the Welbeck Publishing Group.
Offices in London, 20 Mortimer Street, London, W1T 3JW,
and Sydney, 205 Commonwealth Street, Surry Hills, 2010.
www.welbeckpublishing.com

Design © 2023 OH Editions
Text © 2023 Liberty Phi
Illustrations © 2023 Evi O. Studio

A CIP catalogue record for this book is available from the British Library.

ISBN 978-1-91431-799-6

Publisher: Kate Pollard
Editor: Sophie Elletson
In-house editor: Matt Tomlinson
Designer: Evi O. Studio
Illustrator: Evi O. Studio
Production controller: Jess Brisley
Printed and bound by Leo Paper

10 9 8 7 6 5 4 3 2 1